Amish Women

by

Alma Hershberger

1-881061-00-0

Expression
of
Appreciation

The author wishes to sincerely express her appreciation
and thanks to all the Amish women from far and near
who donated their time to her to make this book
possible, or contributed to the book.

Hope this will answer many people's questions about
the Amish women and realize that the Amish people are
real people too.

Let there be peace among us all.

ALMA HERSHBERGER

1-881061-00

Autographed copies can be obtained by writing to:

ALMA HERSHBERGER
P.O. BOX 375
DANVILLE, OHIO   43014-0375
614-599-7072

Information about ordering other books about the Amish can be obtained from the order form in the back.

Typeset by Round Table Inc.
4686 Derby Road
Kalona, Iowa   52247

1-881061-00

AUTHOR

Alma Hershberger

ILLUSTRATION BY:

Velma Beale

Published by
Art of Amish Taste
P.O. Box 375
Danville, Ohio   43014-0375
ISBN 1-881061-00-0

1-881061-00

149332

This page is dedicated to the artist Thelma Beale, to do with what ever pleases her.

The Amish woman surrounded by her family which illustrates her influence in life.

1-881061-00

Preface

AMISH WOMEN

Through the years after leaving the Amish tradition, I have been asked numerous times, "What is it like to be an Amish Woman?"

This book was written to enlighten as well as to entertain those that are interested in studying different ethnic cultures.

The stories contained in this book are written about a few of the Amish women I have met and some of the women I have known. Their names have been changed to protect their privacy.

The book is about good times, bad times and fun times in the lives of the Amish women that have dedicated their lives to what they have been taught. Living life as they think it should be lived.

1-881061-00

8

1-881061-00

Table of Contents

1-881061-00

1-881061-00

AN AMISH WOMAN

An Amish woman's head of hair was given to her for her glory.

Her mind is to think and teach her children right from wrong.

Her eyes are to see that her children do no evil.

Her nose is to smell the aroma of the food she prepares. To know when her baby needs a diaper changed.

Her mouth is to give her family affectionate kisses.

Her ears are to listen when a child cries in need.

Her hands are filled with tender loving care and hard work.

Her heart beats for peace.

Her knees are used to kneel in prayer for the whole world.

Her feet carry her to take care of her responsibility.

Her body is given unto her husband with love. She gives birth for an extra pair of helping hands on the farm.

She is a walking flower in full bloom. At the end the flower will die. She leaves good memories behind; Her family will miss her.

LIST OF STATES AND TOWNS WHERE ALMA'S AMISH FAMILIES ARE EXPLODING IN AMERICA AND CANADA

ALABAMA
Talladega
CANADA
Aylmer, ON
Dryden, ON
Mission, BC
Mossley, ON
Mt. Elgin, ON
Salford, ON
Pickle Lake, ON
COLORADO
Arvada
Burlington
Canon City
Denver
Golden
Littleton
Penrose
Pueblo
Sugar City
DELAWARE
Dover
Hartly
FLORIDA
Boynton Beach
Bradenton
Eaton Park
Eustis
Ocala
Orlando
Sarasota
Zephyrhills
GEORGIA
Dallas
ILLINOIS
Arthur
Sullivan
INDIANA
Berne
Bristol
Elkhart
Foraker
Goshen
Indianapolis
Kokomo

LaGrange
Ligonier
Loogootee
Middlebury
Millersburg
Nappanee
New Paris
North Manchester
Rome City
Shipshewana
Syracuse
Topeka
Vevay
Wollcottville
Warsaw
IOWA
Bloomfield
Fairbank
Hazleton
Independence
Kalona
Riverside
KANSAS
Abbyville
Burrton
Garnett
Haven
Haysville
Hutchinson
Junction City
Meade
Welda
KENTUCKY
Boaz
Crofton
Fancy Farm
Gradyville
Guthrie
Marion
Mayfield
Trenton
MARYLAND
Owings

MICHIGAN
Battle Creek
Burr Oak
Centerville
Grand Rapids
Mio
Three Rivers
White Pigeon
MINNESOTA
Blackduck
Chatfield
St. Charles
Utica
MISSOURI
Garden City
Jamesport
Paris
NEW YORK
Highland
OHIO
Alliance
Andover
Baltic
Berlin
Charm
Cincinnati
Danville
Dover
Dundee
Fresno
Hartville
Hicksville
Hilliard
Kinsman
Lucas
Middlefield
Millersburg
Newark
North Canton
Oxford
Plain city
Reynoldsburg
Rogers
Sugarcreek
Uniontown
Wilmot

cont. on page 92

12

1-881061-00

THEIR HISTORY

The Amish women most certainly include the historical culture with their roots from Germany and Switzerland. A young couple traveled across the sea on an unknown ship, in the Seventeenth Century, to free themselves from the torture their people were faced with, due to their religion. The young man, her husband, died at sea. The young widow, was Barbara Yoder. She arrived with nine children, four sons and five daughters to raise in the free country, America.

Amish women as we know them today, take on a new appreciation, because one becomes aware that the proper definition of Amish women must also include inescapable conscious awareness of their history as preserved in the form of their people. Many people have been handed their tradition down through the generations, the historical and cultural aspects of one people, and it is therein that we find the true value and importance of these courageous people.

Their history know no bounds and continues to march into the future. Since the days the Amish ancestors migrated across the wild country leaving land they developed behind as they moved on and others moved in as their people continued to grow. Otherwise forgotten traces of the feelings and experiences with our Amish people would have passed.

There are romantic as well as tragic memories preserved for us all. The pain and beauty both resound. Horses' feet clip clopping along with the buggy wheels and the lyrics touch the depth of our memories and emotions. The Amish country graciously opened their doors in their area so people may attune to their way of life and capture the moments now in passing.

It is now in the hands and hearts of our young Amish women to continue in their fashion. These people continue to live the historical way for its their tradition in religion. We as the appreciative audience, have the responsibility to protect the Amish people who are striving so hard to continue living the historical style in modern times.

Amish woman is a flower blooming in the Amish country in the history and in the presence of their people. She is the flower of the true humanity and blooms with love, pain, beauty and sorrow. She is a flower cultivated with a gentle touch, with a hand from heaven.

God created woman to please a man, for a companion and to give birth, a flower that radiates a glow of love for her people and hope for a better future for the young and for the generations to come. God, created a flower that may touch each of our lives in it's own special way.

1-881061-00

AMISH WOMEN'S HEAD

The Amish women are required to wear a head covering due to their religious traditions. When the babies are born, the mothers will make a material covering for the baby girls and a little head veil will be worn everyday until she grows to be an adult. The mother will teach her child not to cut her hair, and pray she will accept Jesus Christ's laws, when she reaches the age of accountability.

The Principle For Wearing The Veiling Is Based On The Bible (King James Version).

But I would have you know, that the head of every man is Christ; and the head of the woman is the man; and the head of Christ is God. **1 Cor. 11:3.**
This verse speaking on the "head" means "Authority."

Now I praise you, brethren, that ye remember me in all things, and keep the ordinances, as I delivered them to you. **1 Cor. 11:2.** These ordinances are intended to be kept. They are not something merely to talk about. They should be literally observed and kept.

The Amish believe that the man is appointed head of the house. This is not to give him license to be cruel and overbearing or even unreasonable. The man is to be pleasant, patient and understanding. He is not to be a tyrant, but the leader, the head of the house and family. He is responsible for making the final decisions. The man should love and be faithful to God and to his family.

1-881061-00

AMISH WOMEN

The young are taught and trained as they are developing into adulthood to ready themselves for future homemakers and to obey God's will.

Reasons For Wearing Material Head Covering:

1 Cor. 11:6-16 *For if the woman be not covered, let her also be shorn: but if it be a shame for a woman to be shorn or shaven, let her be covered.*
7) For a man indeed ought not to cover his head, forasmuch as he is the image and glory of God: But the woman is the glory of the man.
8) For the man is not of the woman; but the woman of the man.
9) Neither was the man created for the woman; but the woman for the man.
10) For this cause ought the woman to have power on her head, because of the angels.
11) Nevertheless, neither is the man without the woman, neither the woman without the man, in the Lord.
12) For as the woman is of the man, even so is the man also by the woman; but all things of God.
13) Judge in yourselves: is it comely that a woman pray unto God uncovered?
14) Doth not even nature itself teach you, that if a man have long hair, it is a shame unto him?
15) But if a woman have long hair, it is a glory to her: For her hair is given her for a covering.

These are the verses that the Amish in every denomination go by when it comes to wearing a covering. The different denominations have their own style, but with similarities. The Mennonities, you may recognize immediately because of the difference in style.

One day, I stopped to see an old Amish friend, she was an Old Order member, the lady was pressing one of the little girls coverings with a knife, she said; "Boy, would I like to get my hands on the man that thought of this." I could very well see her point. Wearing a covering is one thing, having to press pleats for a design is extra work for a mother of ten children. Her valuable time could be used spending it with her family.

When it comes to the face, the Amish women do not wear face make up or nail polish. They will use hand lotion and moisture cream to keep from having dry skin problems.

1-881061-00

AMISH WOMEN

LITTLE GIRLS

The Amish children are taught to help around the house and out in the barn taking on responsibility regardless of the size of the hands they have.

The Amish girls are mothers helpers, they learn how to change diapers for the baby. The messy diapers are placed in a bucket of water to be soaked. Diapers would be washed out on every washing day. When I was five and six years old my sisters and myself were mom's helpers, washing the stinky diapers out by hand, before they were thrown in the clothes washer to be washed. We would pick up the corner of a diaper, try to shake the stool out so we wouldn't have to touch it. If it didn't shake loose we had to take our hand and lift it off the diaper. This was so gross but it had to be done and the more we did it the less gross it became. The Amish don't use diaper service or pampers like many modern people use today, causing a big problem with our waste disposal in our environment. Diaper service and pampers is like throwing money out the window. The Amish are very conservative. One Amish motto is, "Haste makes waste." Do you realize that Jesus said, "...*Gather up the fragments that remain, that nothing be lost.*" **St. John 6:12**.

The young girls are taught to help with milking the cows by hand. There are some cows with smaller teats and they tend to kick when a larger pair of hands try to milk them.

1-881061-00

AMISH WOMEN

Young children have smaller hands and can milk the smaller teats easy, without pinching the cow. Hobbles were always put on the cows legs to protect the little girls trying to take on a new responsibility. Milking cows by hand is an exercise that builds a body up. Arms are built strong to the point where the girls could wrestle with their brothers and beat them. Yes! Amish girls enjoy wrestling with their brothers. This is part of being young.

Every morning the breakfast dishes are done before eight o'clock, before the girls leave for school. Teenage girls would mix up a batch of bread dough for mom to continue after the children went to school. The children would look forward to having warm fresh baked bread after school. The girls hands take a beating, milking, washing dishes, dirty diapers, sweeping the floors and working in bread dough. Their hands are trained to take on a very delicate job, pinching a pie crust edge, washing eggs or caring for a new born babe.

The Behinders and the Old Order children are taught the Amish language and German is used in their church. The little boys and girls don't know any other language until their first day of school.

At age six the innocent children are sent off to school. There, in many cases, they are exposed to a strange new language for the first time. The new language is English. English is not spoken in the Amish home and unless they are exposed quite often to the English speaking people. They don't learn to speak English until they enter school. Although the Amish people pay property taxes that support the local public schools,

LITTLE GIRLS

they build their own schools, maintain the schools, and pay the teachers from their own resources in most areas. This practice has come about for many very obvious reasons, one of which is to protect them from the influence of the world. With their own schools the children can be taught in their own tradition without exposing them to things they feel are sinful, also, protecting them from discrimination due to their religious beliefs.

Lets talk about the lady I met, her name was Katie. She is seventy-nine years old. She spoke to me about her first day of school as if it were yesterday. She was raised in Old Order Amish in the State of Kansas. The first year, Katie went to Dodge City, Kansas school. It was a public school. She had never been exposed to the English language until she went to school. She didn't know the English language or understand it. Katie was an innocent six year old child sitting at her school desk, watching and listening to her teacher, but she didn't understand the tongue the teacher spoke. One day not long after school had begun, the teacher walked over to her and Katie received the teachers hand across her face. Little Katie sat at her desk and cried, in confusion, not knowing why the teacher had struck her. This act by the teacher hurt little Katie very much, both physically and mentally. The teacher did this several times throughout the year that Katie attended this school. Do you think, that possibly this teacher had a problem or did she not understand that this child had not been exposed to English at home and that this was her first experience in the English speaking world?

1-881061-00

AMISH WOMEN

Due to experiences such as the one with little Katie, this is probably why the Amish have stood up to the various states and fought for their own schools.

The Amish do believe that it is very important that their children be educated in Reading, Writing, Spelling and Arithmetic. They don't believe that sports should be included as their studies, but they do play ball at recess, for relaxation and exercise.

When I went to school, our people did not salute the American flag and did not have prayer in school. They believe prayers should be held in closed closets, in other words, teachings of religion are done at home. The home is their closed closet.

1-881061-00

AMISH WOMEN

TEENAGE GIRLS

When the Amish have teenage children, they teach them to the point where most of their battle of raising a child is over. Teenagers are young adults doing a young man or woman's job. When the young child wants to help, the Amish born mother begins teaching the children with love, patience and supervision. Children are given responsibility early in their lives and this is why Amish teenagers are capable of handling the adult responsibilities.

Many English people (people that don't speak the Amish language) will call on an Amish girl for help due to their reputation of being honest, are good with children, good employees and reliable. When I travel across this beautiful country in the settlements where Amish people live, I find many young teenage girls taking on a variety of jobs in restaurants, factories, general stores, bakeries, dry goods, quilt shops, gift shops, any place where there is an opportunity to do something they can to help, and ultimately enjoy the work. Some will clean house, but so many of the girls find it more rewarding to do other jobs than to clean house for the English. The young girls will help their own people when a mother has a new baby. Some will be live in maids from Monday through Friday. However today these girls are hard to find because the Amish parents have allowed their girls to work in other fields of labor of their choice. The girls could go home every night rather than be gone all week.

The young girls are not allowed to date until they are sixteen years old. A sixteen year old girl will get to socialize with the young folks on Sunday nights. She has reached the accountability age. The young folks do get together on Sunday evenings. Old Order Amish have church every other Sunday. Whenever they have church the young folks will get together in the evening about eight o'clock for a singing.

In 1990, I visited the Choteau, Oklahoma Amish. I was invited to their singing at my cousins home. Their singing was in German and English. This group had two different song books. They had their tables set up so some could sit at the table or sit on rows and rows of benches. Since I carry music in my heart all the time this was a total enjoyment to me. They had their friends, neighbors and families plus the young folks. These Old Order Amish could really sing, because it came from the heart. They don't use instruments in their church or singings, it is all vocal. A lot of the songs they sang were in German and were very familiar to me since I was raised with the Amish. Of course, I knew all the English songs too. The tones of all the high and low notes of every voice was really beautiful. It's been a long time since I've enjoyed the singing like they had and they made me feel welcome. They asked me if I had a special song, and I told them I enjoyed them all. Everyone took turns announcing their choice by book and page number, at the end of each song. Around eleven, the young folks left and went their way.

We sang a couple more songs and we visited for about an hour with the friends, cousins and neighbors before departing. It was a refreshing fun time that we were blessed with sharing. I couldn't believe it was midnight!

1-881061-00

AMISH WOMEN

A young girl may meet a gentlemen at the young folks singing and the young man may ask her if he may take her home. Then after a couple of dates, they may decide to go steady. When they decide to announce an engagement, they announce it on a church day, after the sermon. The man and woman will depart before the singing starts to end the service. Everyone knows now that there will be a wedding in the next week.

When my family lived in Iowa, the weddings were on Thursday. Most of the Old Order Amish have their weddings on Thursday. I have learned since, there are very few settlements that have weddings on a Tuesday. The wedding plans are made by the bride and her parents. My family always invited the church, the groom and the bride's family. The family could plan on 200 to 300 people to feed. When I was making my wedding plans I asked for the groom's family addresses, so I could mail out their invitations. My mother-in-law to be, told me that in Holmes County ,Ohio, they don't usually invite the family of the groom. "What?" I asked, "I was taught that when you get married you should treat both families alike and I won't consider any other way." On our wedding day we had 275 people in attendance. A family from Indiana came to our wedding and they thanked me for inviting them. One cousin came to me and said, "I wanted to come to the wedding so much, so when I was invited I wasn't going to miss it for the world." There was a cousin, I didn't know her, who told my fiancé that I was not good enough for him. Much later she came to me and told me she was sorry, for it's the other way around. The Amish families do have their differences, they are just real people like you and I.

TEENAGE GIRLS

The Old Order Amish wedding is quite an event. The bride usually mails the invitations out the very next day, (Monday), after their engagement announcement. The bride's family and friends will clean house top to bottom. They will plan their menu and start the preparation of the food. They will serve a full coarse meal consisting of fried chicken, mashed potatoes, noodles, salads, bread, vegetables, sweetheart pudding, date pudding, fruit, cakes, and pies. That same evening, they prepare another meal for the youth group that gathers every Sunday evening, and whom will be singing on the wedding night.

The upstairs of the house is open to the guests and one room is opened for a place for the wedding gifts. Gifts are placed on the bed and on the floor after the bed is full. After supper and the singing is over, the newly married couple will open their gifts.

The wedding takes place year round, from January through December. The Old Order Amish through the Beachy brides may wear a beautiful plain fabric. No fancy lace wedding dress, but a new Sunday dress made for a special day. The bride will make her own dress with assistance from her mother.

Two couples will be chosen for witnesses. The girls have a special blue dress for the wedding day. The Amish believe that blue is for happiness. Weddings are very happy occasions and they are an all day event. The bride and her attendants usually wear blue dresses with the capes and aprons matching the dresses. Their veils for the head are made according to man's

1-881061-00

AMISH WOMEN

tradition. The wedding clothes are so they may be worn many Sundays to come.

The groom will have a new three piece suit consisting of trousers, vest, jacket with a new white shirt. He will be all decked out for this special occasion and will wear the suit for many more Sunday Church services.

The horse and buggy Amish and Beachy church wedding is usually in order like their traditional Sunday service. The church service starts at nine A.M. with singing. A sermon is given on marriage. About ten o'clock a big mixing bowl of homemade cookies is passed for the small children to help prevent the children from becoming so hungry and restless, in the Old Order church.

After the main sermon is given the preacher will sit down, and service will be turned over to the other preacher, deacon and bishop for their witness. The young couple will be asked to come forward and the marriage vows are given to them. The couple will return to their seats. The service will continue and they will close the service with singing at twelve P.M.

After closing, everyone will stay seated until the bride and groom with their witnesses, stand up and leave to go to the house where the reception is to be held. The congregation will follow.

In some Amish communities, you may find young boys and girls that don't belong to the Amish church who will go into town on Saturday night and change into modern clothes. Some have to sow a few wild oats before they decide to settle down.

1-881061-00

AMISH WOMEN

THE CHURCHES

At one time Plain City, Ohio was known to be a large Amish settlement. Not so many years ago they had one hundred and fifty, Old Order Amish families. I asked a gentleman from this community why he left the Old Order and he told me, "Some would study the Book of Life and decided, the church wasn't spiritual enough. Much depended on what the Bishop said and not enough on the Good Book. Some of the Old Order didn't teach you to study or read the Bible. Some communities don't have Bible Study either." The Beachy through the Mennonites have Sunday School and church every Sunday morning and evening with prayer meetings on Wednesday night. Services in the Beachy Church are preached in the Amish language so the children can understand the preaching. The Mennonites use the English in services and for teaching Gods word. The Old Order uses High German which in some communities don't teach. The children can't understand the preaching that lasts for about three hours.

When a family moved to Indiana from Iowa, they started to study the Bible and decided to go to the Beachy church. The father in Iowa, decided to make a trip to Indiana to visit his children. On his visit, he asked, "Why are you leaving the church?" The son replied, "We have been reading and studying our Bible and decided to change." "Well, don't read your Bible so much and listen to your Bishop more," said the father. The son went to the other room, picked up his Bible, returned to the room they were in and laid it on the table saying, "If you don't want me to read the Bible, you take the book with you." The father walked to the table, paused, looking down at the Book of Life. But he couldn't take the Good Book with him.

Old Order Amish don't have Bible Study, and many of the people wanted to go to a church where they felt more of a spiritual environment. Some went to the Beachy, Conservative and Mennonites. These Amish are more modern, plus they have automobiles, unlike the others.

Some of the Old Order moved away because the parents didn't want their children to follow their friends and be living in an environment where their friends have left the Old Order Church. Some of them looked for another Amish settlement nearby, others moved to a new area completely, an area they felt would be a suitable atmosphere to begin a new community, safer, away from the influence of the modern thinking ways.

1-881061-00

AMISH WOMEN

CATHOLIC TURNED AMISH

A young lady raised Catholic as a child in Knoxville, Iowa, who grew up without her mother after losing her at a very young age, grew up and started dating as a young girl would. One day in the early 1970's, she met a young man. The young man was from Bloomfield, Iowa, he had left his Amish home and traditions.

They dated and fell in love. He asked her if she would marry him? She said, "Yes", and they were married.

In later years the young man couldn't sleep nights. Leaving the Amish, began to be an obsession for him. His wife heard about the Amish from her husband and thought it would be an interesting life. They went back to see if the Amish would take them into the Old Order Church. The Amish Bishop said, "Yes, but they were giving the young lady a grace period of one year."

When the young girls and boys become a member they have to get into a training session, every other Sunday for six months. In their counseling they learned all the Amish traditions and rules.

The young man started his training immediately and was baptized into the Amish Church. For six months after he was baptized into the Amish Church, his wife was still driving around in her little red convertible car and wearing shorts. He was wearing his traditional Amish clothes and growing whiskers.

1-881061-00

AMISH WOMEN

After her one year grace period she decided to join the Amish church with her husband. The Old Order Amish preacher explained the rules and traditions to her in English so she would understand. She didn't understand the Amish language, or German. The Amish have no written language. The German language is used for the church services. They went to the Old Order Amish Church for ten years. However, she was getting very unhappy with this church because the women wouldn't speak anything but their own language. She did not understand their speaking tongues. In 1987, they decided to go to another Amish church named the Bethal. This church has Sunday School to teach their people the Bible, and they have a Sunday sermon, on every Sunday in their church building. This group also uses the English language, they say, God, understands English too.

Today the lady is happier because, as she said, "I really needed the teaching of the Bible, I have learned how to make the clothes for my family, I have learned how to garden through books. With help from my husband, I have learned how to cook." She would call on her mother-in-law. The whole family including her husband helped her. When she met her husband, all she knew was hot dogs and potato chips on a plate for dinner. Today she can make a full meal for her Amish family. "If it hadn't been for the language barrier," she said, "I would have stayed with the Old Order Church, because I enjoyed the lifestyle."

CATHOLIC TURNED AMISH

1-881061-00

AMISH WOMEN

HELPING HANDS

Ohio has the largest Amish settlement in the United States of America. The Amish are a large family. Holmes County, Ohio, a beautiful area has more than twenty churches in this Amish community.

The very strict church is the Swartzentrubers or the Behinders. They are as natural as possible regarding material things. No gravel on their drive ways and the women's clothing is dark. You can usually pick these women out immediately.

The Old Order, is the next step to more liberal. They try to keep their farm homes looking very nice so their neighborhood is more appealing. Some of their farms are very attractive. You may find white painted buildings, their transportation is horse and buggy. Electric is not used, neither are telephones or tractors for convenience.

The next step is the New Order Amish Church. These people have the telephone, electric, and tractors however they still travel with the horse and buggy.

Then its the Beachy, Bethal, Mary Nathan, Conservative and on through to the Mennonite churches. The Beachy through the Mennonite churches do use the automobile for their transportation. The women all have a different dress code, similar in style, except for some of the Conservative and the Mennonite congregations. These women are permitted to buy their clothing ready made. These people are all in the Amish family with different titles for their church groups. Tradition plays a big role in their religion.

1-881061-00   37

When my family moved from Iowa in 1951, to Ohio, we learned that the people in Ohio, help the unfortunate people in many countries. It was announced that a meat canner would be in the Hartville community to can meat to help feed the hungry people on the other side of our world. All my sisters who were available went with mother to cut the meat off the beef bones and cut it into chunks. This was my first experience, helping to feed the needy people on the other side of this world. I never saw so many old and young women get together to cut up meat to be canned. The young Amish boys and men too gave a helping hand that day. At the end of the day I really felt good about this new experience, giving a helping hand for the needy people.

Over the years the cost of shipping canned food was too expensive for the community, Today, the Amish have a new way of giving a helping hand to the unfortunate people. Different domination have missionaries in other countries. This is the day when everybody will put their differences behind them and all work together to give to their mission a special helping hand. On the Saturday, of Labor Day weekend, you can go to one of the biggest auctions I have ever seen, located in Mt. Hope, Ohio, it is known as the HAITI SALE.

The year I went to the Haiti sale, they had a couple of tents up outside the auction barn. The big tent had several ice cream freezers where they serve the homemade ice cream and made cotton candy, at one end. The other end was filled with picnic tables so people could sit down to eat and rest a while. In the

38

AMISH WOMEN

other tent the Amish women had brought in the baked goods, there were cookies, cakes, sweet rolls, pies, breads. You could purchase these items for your weekend meals.

Near the auction building in a small tent filled with quilts, made by all the Amish women throughout the year for this most special event. I amazed and admired the ten rows of quilts all handmade by the Amish women and girls. Colors like the rainbow in every hue, from soft pastels, to deep blues. Any woman's dream comes true.

There were unlimited amounts of woodcraft items, with shelves of all shapes, and in all sizes, oak desks, and wood furniture in all kinds of wood, too many to list.

Outside, they had swing sets, play houses and outdoor furnishings of every kind. So much that I can't begin to describe to you.

It is an auction with so many specially made things that you can spend the whole day, just browsing. A wonderful sale for Christmas shoppers, and the funds go to support a good cause.

They had two auctioneers going at the same time. One on the inside and one on the outside. The livestock was out-side in the auction corral. The animals were beautiful.

The money the sale brought in would be taken over to Haiti, in person by the one that was nominated.

I was visiting with one New Order Amish lady, when she said, "This is how I imagine what heaven is going to be. Everyone will be together no matter what church you go to. It's what is in the heart that counts."

1-881061-00

THE HARNESS MAKER

When an Amish women is past the age of twenty-four
years of age and single, she is considered an old maid.

In 1989, the Plain City , Ohio, the horse and buggy
Amish community, had eight unmarried women past the
age of twenty-four years old. In addition, there were
four couples with children and three widowed ladies
left in this Amish church.

It was a beautiful sunny and brisky day when I stopped
to see Rachel. One of the old maids' at her place of
business.

When driving into her driveway she and a sister have a
cute white house with a neat looking yard on the left
side of the driveway. At the end of the driveway they
have a small barn for their horse and buggy. On the
right side is a small white building where Rachel has a
leather shop.

When you walk into her shop she has a work table on
one side and one in the center with two big wheels
hanging from the ceiling loaded with her hand tools
very neatly organized. The building had plenty of
windows to provide her with a lot of natural light for
her work. Rachel's manual tractor was sitting between
two windows where she depended on good natural
light.

Rachel was in her sixties, she mounts herself on an old
manual tractor seat, puts her feet on heavy homemade
block peddles, providing the power for a massive

leather sewing machine, which was formerly run by electric.

Rachel described how she learned to cut patterns out of brown paper bags and newspaper. "Give me a sample of something that you want, and I will make it for you." She said, continuing, "I rely on the English people for work today. Since most of our people have moved away or left the church. There are many Amish women who work making harness. They have a harness making reunion annually."

"Our reunion was held in Arthur, Illinois last year." she commented.

Rachel Miller will repair saddles, harness, bridles and will make new ones. On the day I visited her shop she was making a leather tool belt that a customer had ordered.

Rachel, is physically in good health and will continue working for twenty more years, so long as she is physically able to do it. She found this more satisfying work than cleaning house for people.

Don't you have to admire this lady to take on her very own harness shop?

1-881061-00

THE HARNESS MAKER

44

AMISH WOMEN

UNLIMITED LOVE

Vernon and Laura Coblentz were married in 1958, in
Hartville, Ohio, and later they decided to move to
Milroy, Indiana. They had six children. Laura always
wanted to have more children, for some reason she did
not conceive again after the birth of their sixth child.

Living in the same community, Leroy and Mary Jane
Kemp had eleven children, their ages ranging from five
months to sixteen years.

The Kemp's lived on a dairy farm, in a house with two
bedrooms. The family was very poor. Mary Jane, a
beautiful women always carried a big smile no matter
how much or how little she had. She did anything she
could to help others.

The year of 1985, the last week of January, the Kemps
received word that their uncle had passed away. The
funeral was to be on the last day of January and was
about one hundred thirty miles from Milroy, Indiana.
They managed to get a van load of friends together. A
total of nine people went on the trip. Mary Jane and
Leroy decided to take the four year old son along to the
funeral. It was snowing all day and the roads were in
very bad condition by night fall. On their way home
traveling on a state road, an eighteen wheeler truck
went into a slide and jack-knifed meeting the van load
of nine people. The eighteen wheeler trailer landed on
top of the van. It killed four people instantly, the
others were taken to the nearby hospital. Mary Jane,
the mother of eleven children was killed. Leroy and the
four year old son were still alive.

1-881061-00   45

The Amish people went to the Kemp's home like Amish communities do, across this country to give their moral support and a helping hand. The children knew Laura Coblentz and were close to her because she was giving their mother a hand with the work every week and had become like a second mother to the Kemp children.

Because the Kemp's were so poor, Laura had to borrow warm winter clothes to wear to their mother's funeral. Leroy, their father died two weeks later. The four year old was released from the hospital after two weeks. Vernon and Laura picked the boy up from the hospital and took him to his home.

The second funeral was planned for the children's father. After the funeral the Coblentz's went home.

The next morning, Laura was preparing breakfast for her family. Before she sat down to eat, she told her family, "I have to go back over to the children." She left without eating her breakfast that morning. Laura said, "I never went back home to my house. I stayed because the children didn't want me to leave." After the funeral the sixteen year old boy told Vernon, "I don't know where I'm going to get money to get groceries."

Vernon and Laura had four sons married, and two girls still living with them. A couple of weeks passed after the funeral when the Coblentz's decided to move in with the Kemp children. This was hard for the two Coblentz girls because they each had their own bedrooms. When the two girls were told of the decision, they went out on the porch, sat down on the

46

steps and cried their hearts out. They were being affected by the sad chain of events too. Although not as drastically as the Kemp children were.

The Kemps had a two bedroom house. The living room was very small. However, the kitchen was good size for a big table and a work table with cupboards. The cupboards had a variety of dishes none of which was a complete set.

The Kemp family had run a dairy farm with twenty cows to milk and a lot of chores that had to be done. This was a factor that brought about the decision to move to the Kemp farm with the Kemp children.

One bedroom had two double beds. Vernon and Laura slept in the small bedroom in a half bed and the little children slept in their own beds. A double mattress was used for the bed for the Coblentz girls. Every night, the mattress was pulled out on the kitchen floor. In the morning the mattress was put away, setting it up between the two double beds. Can you imagine how hard it would be to leave a comfortable home, your own beds and live as they did? Just imagine!

The Kemps were very poor trying to do with what they had. After the parents had died the people heard about the poor situation on the farm. The different Amish communities from all over the United States and the English people (non Amish speaking) pitched in to help with donations. They had two showers that were published in the Amish paper, THE BUDGET, located in Sugarcreek, Ohio. They received quilts, blankets, diapers, and money.

One of Vernon's business associates, (not of the Amish), gave Vernon a check in the amount of $600.00, to help the orphaned children. Laura would bake bread three times a week, she made eight loaves at a time, this was a total of twenty-four loaves weekly.

Vernon and Laura made plans to build a seven bedroom house for their new family with money received through donations. Laura said, "I guess God was saving me for the eleven children. After I had my sixth child, I wanted more but I didn't know why I couldn't get pregnant again." When they made plans to build the new house, the Amish have what they call a frolic. The Amish came in by van loads helping to build the new house they were needing so desperately. Some of the women came to help. They sanded and varnished the woodwork.

Laura said, "I really don't know how I would have done everything without my girls' help. The girls have grown to be close to their new brothers and sisters. We are all a big happy family today."

When the youngest girl started school, she came home and said, "The children said you're not my real mother, I just don't believe it." she said, as she ran off to play. She never questions it. We talk about it in her presence now and she knows about it from hearing us talk, of things that had taken place after her mother and father died. We do not try to hide the truth from her.

The older children are married and they thank us for their training. The middle boys are working out, while

1-881061-00

AMISH WOMEN

the girls are doing the farm chores mornings and evenings.

The two girls are dating Laura's nephews. Grandpa said, "My nieces are dating my nephews." They all had to laugh on that statement.

Isn't this a great way of life? Vernon and Laura Coblentz, and their two young daughters sure had to give up a lot to help these children. But the love they gave the children, will be showered back with love in return, from these children for the rest of their life.

Even the children's services couldn't have done a better job finding these children parents like the Coblentz's. The children were afraid they would be split up. Laura promised the children, they would never have to worry about splitting up. No child should have to leave their brothers or sisters in any case. Its too bad the children's services can't work in this manner, for the good of all. Laura said, "The children are very close to each other just like brothers and sisters should be."

1-881061-00

AMISH WOMEN

AMISH WOMEN

It is overwhelming to the people from the city as they
visit the Amish country. The country is just
astonishing, it's just so different in many ways. People
are embraced by unfamiliar sights and sounds
surrounded by a culture they barely fathomed still
carrying on the old traditions as their ancestors did
years ago.

A lady was taking a tour with her friends through the
small town of Berlin, Ohio in the heart of Amish
country. When I met her, I asked her, "What do you
think about Amish country?" She responded, "It is
beautiful!" Then she came up to me and whispered, "I
have never seen Amish people before and the first time
I saw them, I saw three women walking along the road,
I thought they were nuns, they were dressed in plain
clothes, I am fascinated with the way they live and
dress. It is like going back in time."

The Amish women are not Nuns but women who dress
according to their man made tradition. I replied, "Yes,
I know, my friend told me that, but I had never seen
Amish people before or a horse and buggy. I'm having
an enjoyable time." I stated, "Good, I hope you have a
safe trip home." She thanked me and walked away,
smiling.

There are many people from the city that see the Amish
women for the first time, wear the same expression as
this lady did who was touring the Amish countryside,
due to the Amish dress code, wearing the black bonnet,
white veil, ankle or mid calf length dresses, black
shawls, stockings and shoes. The fabrics they use for

dresses are usually of an earthly plain color with no prints.

On the other hand, you have the Beachy Amish through the Mennonites churches, who wear more of a variety. The Conservative Mennonite and Mennonites are allowed prints on their material and wear different styles of clothing. The Old Order Amish are essentially the same across the United States.

There is an Amish lady that lives in the Kalona, Iowa community. She cleaned many houses for the English people, nearby, by the day. When her father took ill, she had wished for a craft and fabric shop at the home farm so she would not have to leave her mother and father. She lived at home and felt responsible for the care of them and she didn't like to leave them alone when they were sick.

When Miss Miller, lost her father. She stayed with her mother to look after her. One week after her father's death through the night the mother called her. Miss Miller went to see what she needed. Her mother asked her if she would put her hand on her heart? She realized, her mother was in need of a doctor's care. After taking her to the doctor, they were told, her mother had a heart problem. Miss Miller was still looking for an opportunity for a business at home so she would not have to leave her mother by herself.

One day an opportunity came along, to buy a craft shop out in the community. She decided to buy it and put it in the back of their house on the farm. Miss Miller, started putting her business together and didn't have to

1-881061-00

AMISH WOMEN

leave her mother's side, or the home. Her mother was
very enthused about the new business and lived to see it
in full operation.

A year later Miss Miller's mother passed away. She
had bought the farm from her parents before they died.
Her brother is a Mennonite farmer and farms the land
on the home farm along with his farm, while she
maintains her busy craft business. She said, in her
energetic way, "It is more rewarding to work in the gift
shop, although, sometimes, it is harder. I love quilts
and quilting is down my alley. I enjoy working with all
the fabrics."

Miss Miller Kountry Kreation Krafts has 4000 bolts of
fabric, 200 quilts, books for adults and children, towels
of all kind, stuffed animals, dolls, craft kits, and wood
crafts. The gifts are numerous and there is something
for the whole family.

When you walk in her shop you may find her sitting at a
quilt frame quilting. She quilts for people that have
ordered special quilts. She had orders for her quilts, a
year ahead. She had her work cut out for her. She is
so pleasant to talk to. If you are ever in her area, I
would suggest that you stop at her shop, you may see
how quilting is done. She will welcome you and help
you get the right fabric for a quilt. She loves fabric,
and, Miss Miller knows her business very well.

1-881061-00

AMISH WOMEN

A MOTHER

Even though I was born and reared in an Amish family, it was my interest to interview other Amish women to conceive their point of view on the Amish style of living. However it didn't take long to realize that we did think a lot alike. Except for their man tradition, I could never follow man traditions, because of; **Colossians 2:8**.

BEWARE LEST ANY MAN SPOIL YOU THROUGH PHILOSOPHY AND VAIN DECEIT, AFTER THE TRADITION MEN, AFTER THE RUDIMENTS OF THE WORLD, NOT AFTER CHRIST.

An Amish woman is like a lady of the last century, quiet in the presence of her husband. She is taught to work by her husband's side in the fields, barn, milk house, along with her own duties in the house, until she has children. Then, the children will help in her place.

When I went to visit an Amish lady in the Amish country she had been married for ten years. Her husband is a wood-working craftsmen, with his own shop, located at their home for his business of income. They have five children ages nine through three months old living in the Nunda, Ohio, community.

In the Nunda, Ohio Amish community family with children in school prepare a luncheon for the one room school once a year. When I stopped to see this lady, she had lunch prepared for the school children. She was serving homemade pizza and ice cream. Yes! Even their children enjoy pizza. Amish children are just as playful and enjoy the same foods as do any other

1-881061-00

children even though they are taught to be serious and accept responsibility at an early age. They are very playful and have lots of fun, just being children.

The father of the home hid little treasures out in the yard for the children to have a treasure hunt, after lunch. Since the Amish do not have telephones in this community, I made arrangements to see her the next morning, while I was there.

Following are the questions I asked her the next morning, and her answers:

Question: What is an Amish woman's duties?

Answer: "I don't feel like I have duties as a wife or a mother. Duties are something you have to do. I am not forced to do anything that I do not want to do. It is my choice to be a mother and a wife. I feel this is a privilege that God gave me a loving husband."

"My husband doesn't ask much of me as far as helping him with his work in the wood-work shop. I try to keep the children and the house so it may be pleasant for him. For a mother and a wife who stays home, it brings much fulfillment to me, to make a house, a home."

"It would break me in pieces if I would have to put my children into a day care center to go to work. The children need their mother at home to give them the Love, Understanding, Teaching and Discipline while they are growing up. Do you really think those children will go to the parents with their problems when

56

1-881061-00

they couldn't be with them to discuss their problems when they were little."

I believe in Titus Chapter 2:3-5.
3) *The aged women likewise, that they be in behaviour as becometh holiness; not false accusers, not given to much wine, teachers of good things;*
4) *That they may teach the young women to be sober, to love their husbands, to love their children,*
5) *To be discreet, chaste, keepers at home, good, obedient to their own husbands, that the word of God, be not blasphemed.*

"I am thankful to my parents for my up bringing since I was born Amish. I have this satisfied feeling about staying home, and caring for my family."

Question: How old are your children when you start training and teaching them?

Answer: "You start at a very young age. At two and three years old you ask them to put their dirty clothes in the hamper. Make their bed. One day, I had a gallon jug with a little milk in it, not full, sitting in the basement. I asked my three year old daughter if she would go to the basement to get the jug of milk for mom? She was surprised, it made her happy. She said, "Ya" She wanted to do something to make me happy. I believe all children want to do good and make their parents happy. You have to give children responsibility. My school age children have duties. The girl does the breakfast dishes before going to school. After school, she rolls up and shakes off the throw rugs, sweeps the floors and put the rugs back in order again. A child needs to be praised and given credit when they do something."

Question: How do you discipline your children?

Answer: "That's a hard question," she replied. "Each child is different. What may work for one may not work for the other. Start at a young age, before one year old. There are different forms. Start by using different tones of voice, when they reach for something like a hot stove, you say, na,na, that's hot. It depends on the age and the will of a child. If their will is stronger to do something that is not good, you treat it accordingly to break that will. You may spank a child. But, you can not treat each child the same. For they are not the same. Never punish a child in anger. Discipline must be done with love. Sometimes, I will sit with a child in a chair and hold it."

"This morning I was rushing around and my children sense it. The four year old was getting fussy, so I picked her up, sat in the rocker, held her, loved her and talked to her until she was alright. Sometimes a child just needs to be loved and talked to. They don't need spanked."

"I don't have a book of rules for my family. I like to make it a happy pleasant home, so when my children grow up they can look back and have happy memories. I'm thankful to God, how wonderful it is to be born into a family where we were wanted and needed."

1-881061-00

Question: Do you have a schedule?

Answer: "Not really. I try to do my laundry on Mondays and Fridays; Wednesdays, I like to try to go home and help mother. Sometimes my sisters will plan to be there to. We take work with us or if mom has something that needs to be done we will help her."

"In the winter, I try to do my main sewing for the family. My girls like to have me make their underwear, because they think they are more comfortable than the ones you buy."

"In Spring, I do my Spring cleaning before it is time to plant garden. Garden planting is a job for the whole family. After planting the garden my nine year old boy came in saying, 'The peas are up Mom.' He was so excited to see that the seeds were growing. Then I knew he was taking an interest in the garden too."

"Fall Cleaning is done after the garden is over."

Question: What is your activity with the family?

Answer: "Wintertime in the evening after a day's work, our family plays games or read after supper. After the weather breaks the children enjoy going fishing at the pond."

"My parents were willing to share the expense of building a cabin beside the pond. The cabin and the pond are between our homes and is in walking distance for our families."

A MOTHER

"Summer time we like to sit on the porch swing and sing after supper. Sometimes on weekends we will go to the cabin for the night. We will fish, build a fire to roast hot dogs or marshmallows."

"Last summer we had the whole family including my married sisters and their families spend the night at the cabin. We all spread sleeping bags over the floor, inside and out on the porch. A couple of the guys slept out under the trees. They all had fun."

Question: Do you wish for a telephone or electricity?

Answer: "No, not really, my husband said, He sure is glad we didn't have a phone. He thought if we had a telephone there would be no peace with the business here at the home. I just send my four year old to mother's with messages. She's my telephone. There wouldn't be peace in a home with a telephone."

Question: What activity do you have in your community?

Answer: "My husband was on the School Board and we pushed to have German Spelling. Through the winter months we had German Spelling every two weeks on a Friday evening. Then we had a spell down. Our Amish school teach high German as a lesson."

"On the German spelling night we would take popcorn and cider along. Afterward, we did this to socialize and communicate together."

1-881061-00

A MOTHER

Question: Is there anything you would like to add that I haven't covered?

Answer: "Yes! Under the Amish is sad to say, but there isn't harmony among all couples. We wouldn't think of leaving because of our faults, that he has or I have. None of us is perfect. When we get married, vows are taken between two people and God. If we try to see the best in each other and live a Christian life anything is possible."

"I believe communication is very important most of the Amish couples do build their marriage on a solid rock, with Christ in the home. It is so sad that so many people do not have the privilege of being raised in a Christian home. I feel a marriage is like a wheel. God is the hub of the wheel. The rim is Love. People are the spokes."

Don't you think this woman has a good out look on family life?

1-881061-00

FAMILY LIFE

While traveling across Kansas, I learned about a family living in the Amish community in Yoder, Kansas. The mother and three daughters were bailing straw for an English lady. The English lady was shipping the baled straw to craft shops across this country. When I stopped to see their setup, Polly Ann, is the name I will give her, she was a cheerful lady and took me out to show me how they did their bailing. The straw is fed in the top of the baler; then, the baler pushes the little bales out at the bottom. She showed me how they have to tie and cut the wire on each bale at the end. She used the cutters to cut the wire. They try to bale eight hundred bales a day.

Polly Ann, lives in the family house on the home farm, with her husband and three daughters. Polly, is the youngest one of five children. Her mother lives in the (Dawny Haus) grandparents house.

Her mother Lillian, takes special care because of her serious illness, Alzheimer's disease. Polly Ann, takes care and watches over her mother. It takes more time than you can imagine. She gets no help from her brothers or sisters-in-law in caring for her mother. It gets harder and almost impossible to leave her mother alone. Her family has to suffer with a heavy load caring for a loved one twenty-four hours a day. They don't get a break away from home due to grandma's illness.

Polly does appreciate her daughters help. They help with Grandma and all the house cleaning, baling the straw, and on washday the girls had been trained before Grandma took ill to hang up the clothes in sunshine or

1-881061-00

AMISH WOMEN

freezing weather. Their clothes dryer is the clothes line. Because they do not believe in using electricity.

Kerosene lights are still used in Amish homes. Some of the chores to be done are to maintain the lights. Usually when the morning dishes are done, the lights are checked to see if the chimneys smoked the night before. If so, they are washed and the lights are filled for that evenings use. The floors are swept, with a broom. Throw rugs are taken outside to be shaken and returned to the proper area.

Monday is washday. Some communities do not allow running water in the house so water must be carried to the house in tremendous amounts for washday. All the clothes and bed linens are gathered on that morning, most homes have gasoline powered motors on the washing machine. They have wringers mounted on top of the machine and they swivel around so that they can be use either direction, from the rinse tub to the basket or from the washer to the rinse tub. The clothes are rinsed twice meaning you have to handle the clothes, at least three times before going to the clothes line. The washer wringer is dangerous. Some of the Amish ladies and girls wear black or blue bandannas. Like head scarves. As they lean over the washer guiding the clothes, back and forth through the wringer, it has caught the scarf, pulling the neck down choking the individual until either she can turn it off or someone else does. It can be a very frightful situation. This happened to both my sisters and me as we were growing up. Another very dangerous thing about the wringer, many hands and fingers get run through it too.

FAMILY LIFE

I remember when I was a child, barely tall enough to reach the clothes lines, we helped mother on wash days. In the winter, when it was freezing weather, I would pick up a piece of cloth that was nice and warm from the rinse water, taking out the clothes-pins to hang it to the line, my fingers got so cold they turned red in a matter of seconds. The piece of cloth would freeze before I had the next piece up. I would quickly put my fingers back into the warm wet clothes in the basket to warm them. I would do this after each piece. After all the clothes in the basket were hung, we'd run back into the laundry to warm our hands in the warm wash water. Oh! did that feel good! Oh my, I want to get back to telling you about Polly.

I stopped in a year later to see Polly Ann, and her lovely family to visit her again. They talked about taking Lillian to the nursing home to give Polly a break. However, Polly's brothers wouldn't agree to it. One brother offered to take care of Lillian's money. This is a sample of how there are people that will work and care for a loved one, beyond their limit and then you have those that are there to grab the money bag and disappear in a few weeks or months. You have this in many families and churches around the world.

There was greed in Jesus' day, when He walked the earth. Do not be deceived into thinking that it does not exist today. The Bible teaches us all that money is evil.

I know God loves Polly Ann and her family for sacrificing so much of their life to their mother. May God Bless Them.

   1-881061-00

AMISH WOMEN

COMMUNITY LOVE

A way of life in caring for a friend, neighbor, and a church member living in a community that is really desirable.

In the Choteau, Oklahoma, community my Aunt Alma, who I was named after had taken sick with cancer. Uncle Al and Aunt Alma had a daughter name Katie, which Aunt Alma had conceived in her later forty's. Katie was a blessing in this home and they thank God for her. They were tickle pink! This is an Amish motto.

Katie is married and has two children living on the home farm, which is the Amish way to care for their elders.

When Aunt Alma took sick and was bed fast. The Old Order Amish women from the community would take turn to go in and stay with Aunt Alma in the evenings to give Katie a break.

Katie had two children that needed her and she needed a break in the twenty-four hours of caring for her mother.

This is the first community I found where church members went in to give a helping hand with understanding, considerate, respect, love and concern for the sick and the sick person's family.

If I would have to give a community a medal award for good deeds according to the Good Book, the award would go to the community of Choteau, Oklahoma.

1-881061-00

AMISH WOMEN

May this be a sample and idea for other churches in other communities to practice.

You may wonder why this is outstanding? Because the people let their heart direct them.

Uncle Al and Aunt Alma were members of the Old Order Amish and their daughter Katie and her family are members of the Mennonite Church. In many communities when one leaves the Old Order Church like Katie decided to do, the Old Order Amish would not consider in helping, but cut all communications with such a person.

These people will follow their heart and let God do the judging.

This community shows love and let God do the judging. This is the greatest gift that I've ever seen since I've known the Old Order Amish in an Amish community.

May this be a sample and idea for other communities and churches to practice. It makes this world a better place to live, when you can show your love for each other. Love is the greatest thing that God gave us.

1-881061-00

AMISH WOMEN

SOCIAL LIFE

The life style the Amish have chosen many wonder with all the manual hard work they do, how do they manage it in their man tradition. Do they have any social life? The Amish do have time for social life.

Their social life is being creative at whatever they do in a variety of things they do. While living in Iowa, the Amish would help each other when it was time for the wheat to be harvested. After the wheat was done on the last day of thrashing, the men decided to get together for an ice cream supper. It was time to relax after the hot days of sweating, working long hours in the wheat fields.

The last day of the threshing, the men folks came home and informed the women where the gathering would be. The women would quickly mix ice cream and fill the ice cream can to take to the long awaited supper. Everyone went to the ice cream social.

Since the Amish don't believe in having insurance with a big insurance company, they have their own insurance with in their community and in God by faith.

They have no control of lightning hitting a building. This is an act of God. If any of their people should lose a house or barn, they will put their share into the cost of the material to rebuild.

When the finances have been arranged, the day to rebuild is planned. This day is called the frolic. The wives plan to go with their men folks and take a

1-881061-00-0

covered dish along to help feed the hundred men on the job.

The women may decide to put a quilt together and some can quilt while others make the dinner. They don't waste much of their time, waste in the Amish is not smart and they don't believe in it. The women enjoy visiting while they are being creative.

When someone in the community needs help with sewing, the women will plan to get together and help. This is a day out for the family or it may be a quilting day for a quilt to be auction at the Haiti sale.

The Old Order Amish have their church in their home. Every other week the neighbors will gather to help clean house top to bottom to ready it for church. This is the opportunity for them to reveal their talent for cooking and baking those items for church, consisting of church cookies, for the little children, mixing peanut butter with marshmallow cream and karo syrup, homemade bread, cakes and pies.

The Amish ladies are known for their delicious food.

1-881061-00
AMISH WOMEN

MID-WIFE

With the cost of living today, two children are plenty
for the average family, but the Amish don't believe in
birth control. This makes the Amish people the fastest
growing group of people in this country today. They
live a life-style; their motto is "They are cheaper by the
dozen."

An Amish family is always excited when they learn that
there is a new baby on the way or has arrived. The
tenth child is as welcome as the first child to an Amish
family. Jesus loves all children red, yellow, black, and
white.

I am visiting a young mother of four, she wants ten
children. All of her babies so far have been delivered at
a mid-wife center, she lives in the Millersburg, Ohio,
area.

My friends among the Amish will give me a call to take
them to visit family, one new Amish wife, and mother
to be, rode with me one day. I asked her if she was
going to use the Mid-Wife Center or the hospital? She
replied, "I will be going to the hospital since it is my
first baby."

Years ago every Amish community was known to have
a mid-wife in their area. Then the Medical Association
decided to push for a law that all babies are to be born
in a hospital in several states. When the new law
passed, they were expecting a baby boom in their
hospital. Instantly they were out-smarted. The Amish
communities in different areas built care centers for

mother-to-be, to deliver their babies. Who said, the Amish are dumb? The Amish are not dumb.

In the seventeenth century the Amish people found this country. They chose to stay here because it was a free country. The Amish people take care of their own people. They train the young to take on responsibility. They have taken on poor land and developed it to be rich land, because they work hard with their manual abilities which is their main tradition. To do as their fore-fathers did.

The Amish people take pride in their land and appreciate their freedom. The Amish people pay taxes just like everybody else plus they don't look for hand outs of the almighty dollar like many people do or run for government assistance.

The Amish people want freedom and don't appreciate the fact that some people are trying to take it away from them. The Amish people are the first to realize that and fear for their freedom. In 1989, the Pennsylvania Amish were under attack when their mid-wife was taken away from them.

Grace Lucille Sykes, is a mid-wife for Western Pennsylvania and Eastern Ohio, Amish women. Lucille, was born in Colorado a beautiful state, a Methodist minister's daughter. Her father chose a church in the state of Washington, where she attended grade school and later college.

Lucille, went to college to be a school teacher, but learned that wasn't for her and decided to get married.

74

1-881061-00

AMISH WOMEN

After she married, she went with her husband James to South Dakota where James received his C.P.A. license.

When the children were old enough to start school, they decided to move their family to Pennsylvania so the children could go to Christian Day School.

When they moved into the midst of the Amish community, Lucille, came to be good friends with the Amish. In 1976, the Amish women trusted her and asked her why she didn't take up mid-wifery. They needed her. She thought about it and she decided she would enjoy this type of occupation.

Lucille, went to Fredricksburg for her training as a mid-wife. She received her training from Mary Ann Hershberger, and worked with a mid-wife in New Wilmington, Pennsylvania. The mid-wife who served the Amish community for nearly half a century was thinking about retiring. While Lucille was serving a two year apprenticeship with the community's mid-wife, she had the pleasure of delivering her first baby in 1976.

The following five years, the demand for Lucille's services grew so tremendously she found it difficult to travel to all the women who needed her. With the Amish belief of not having modern conveniences such as electricity or telephones. It added complications to her job, caring for her expectant mothers.

The Amish people decided to buy a small house in their area and move it to Lucille's back yard in Stoneboro, Pennsylvania. Lucille named her new care center "Cradle Time Birthing Clinic." She joined the Mid-wives Association.

MID-WIFE

1-881061-00

AMISH WOMEN

Lucille, always councils her women, she makes sure that they see a doctor before accepting them. $500.00, is the fee she charges per child delivered, and the hospital will charge at the minimum of about $2,000.00. Lucille sometimes will receive gifts instead of cash. At times, she does not get paid. She realizes many of the families are farmers and they don't have a lot of money.

She received a crib as a payment, which she uses at the Birthing Clinic for the new born babies.

Lucille, has never lost a baby in delivery. There have been complications but she calls for the emergency squad to have them take the mother to the hospital. She gives instructions on how to care for the mother until they get her to the hospital. On one occasion, the paramedics did not follow her instructions, and the baby died. The paramedics were afraid and reported this to Children's Services.

Mercer County Children and Youth Service, began to investigate Mrs. Sykes, Cradle Time Birthing Clinic. A man from Children Services came to her house and told Lucy that she is not to deliver anymore babies, that she was practicing medicine without a license. They began to watch her house. The Amish women continued to come to her for her help. Lucille could not refuse them. She wasn't using medicine and never had.

MID-WIFE

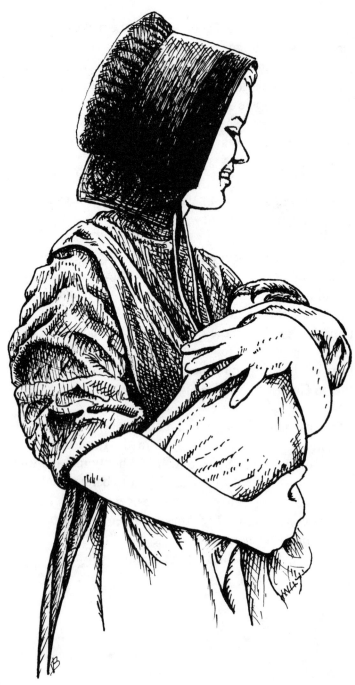

1-881061-00

AMISH WOMEN

Mrs. Sykes, was charged for practicing medicine with out a license and child abuse by the State Police. Lucille did not stop catching the new babies the mothers were delivering.

The mid-wife received support in the battle from the Pennsylvania Midwives Association, a national organization, and the Eastern Ohio and Western Pennsylvania Amish.

The Amish and English decided to stand up for what they believed in. It's called FREEDOM. The people believing in freedom began to show their support for mid-wives and a rally was planned, titled;

FREEDOM OF CHOICE IN CHILDBIRTH

Support Rally For Pennsylvania's Lay Mid Wives Time to speak up and be heard NOW! Please come to this event. Plan to contribute funds, any amount will help. Come and have fun. Please be prompt.

On a Saturday, August 26, 1989 the women planned a 5 PM: POT LUCK DINNER Bring food to share. 7 PM: FUND RAISING DESSERT AUCTION. Net Proceeds Benefit Lucille Sykes Legal Defense Funds. 9 PM: SQUARE DANCING AND OLD TIME MUSIC.

Letters were mailed to newspapers in support for Lucille. When the news traveled across this country, she received letters from individuals giving their support in her time of crisis. Letters came from as far away as California. One came from a woman named Ramona, This is what she had to say;

Dear Ms. Sykes;

After watching your case reported on Inside Edition in July, I am furious. Birth and death are two very private family situations, where strangers and bureaucrats have no place or say. We must stand together to fight these people, and we will win! Society seems to be obsessed with invading the privacy of people. They feel threatened by ignorance, things they do not understand. You would be surprised at how many babies die in hospitals at the hands of idiotic ignorant doctors who do not know what they are doing.

I know that you know what you're doing, for my midwife told me, when I was five months pregnant, that my baby was a boy (without any modern machinery), and, I had a boy.

I don't know you, but I love you and support you all the way! God Bless.

R.M.
Sunnyvale, CA

This next letter is impressive because our Government is giving the young girls the right to use abortion, for birth control today of 1991. Midwives aren't taking lives, they are helping babies enter the world.

Letter to:
Lucille Sykes;

1-881061-00

AMISH WOMEN

Hang in there - God gave us each a talent. **Roman 12:6**, *I commend you for you are what you are, a good person doing a good deed not for one, but for all.*

God be with you and know that I am on your side.

Mennonites and Amish are very good people and you are a good person. What you are doing is saving lives. Around here, (those) giving abortions are taking innocent lives. I would not want to be wearing their shoes. Keep your chin up!

A Friend of Many Mennonites here in PA.
Mifflinburg, PA

Lucille has delivered 700 babies and has never lost a baby in delivery. She received an award (plate) for her outstanding mid-wife services from her community.

D. DAY AT COURT

The D. Day (court), the Amish were coming into Mercer Pennsylvania, in their horses & buggies, entering the town from every direction for the District Justice of The Peace hearing. For the event, Amish from Ohio and other communities arrived in van loads.

The Amish men and women packed the court room, some mothers holding babies, the courtroom was too small to hold all the people who appeared to support their Mid-Wife. The people were standing in the hallway and outside when the judge stated, "Open the window, and let them all see what is happening." The windows were opened, the Amish had filled the courthouse, the outside yard, sidewalks and the coffee shop across the street. It was a day where the Amish were coming out of the wood-work like ants. The judge stared with disbelief. The Amish wanted their Mid-wife back.

Mid-wives defended Lucille, in her day in court. One testified, "Midwives are true protectors of natural childbirth. We're there to protect the natural process of birth. It's really sad that it's become such a big medical event. It's just not necessary. Babies come out. It doesn't have anything to do with medicine."

"**Mid-wives**, is one of the worlds oldest professions. It all started to change in the eighteen hundreds when the doctors found out that they could do this procedure easily and make money from it at the same time. That is when doctors started becoming obstetricians."

The Mid-wife informed the court with concerns regarding infant mortality in the United States. "This country ranks 23rd, in the world in it's infant mortality rate."

"Modern medicine has done nothing to change the fact that doctors are doing all these things to women in labor."

Mid-wife II: "We don't deliver babies, we catch them." She testified.

Mid-wife III: stated, "Parents should be able to make their own choice. If there is a problem, we will transport. Midwives maintain an ongoing agreement with the ambulance service, if a problem arises."

1-881061-00

AMISH WOMEN

"We are not in competition with the doctors we are here to support healthy women and enhance the experience of natural childbirth."

Lucy, as everyone calls her, is dedicated in the work she does. She feels that she offers to her mothers-to-be, a very definite service. They are treated in a very personal and loving manner in the clinic, beginning with the early prenatal visits. She takes extra time for the first-time mom, making a great beginning for not only the new born child but for the parents alike. It is her practice that fathers are to bond immediately with the new babies, as the new mothers do. This practice alone is one that should be practiced in any facility that delivers new borns. With the world in the shape it is in today, we need all the help we can get to raise our children in a loving and tender manner, beginning the very first day. Tenderness and love breeds respect, and thus makes for a wonderful family atmosphere.

Today, Grace Lucille Sykes is still attending the birthing of the beloved babies in her clinic. She has delivered 903 babies to date 1992. She has plans of enlarging the clinic. Don't you think this woman has earned a golden medal?

1-881061-00

AMISH WOMEN

WIDOWS

The Furniture Maker

The Amish have no life insurance, because they believe
they have their insurance in God by faith. When it
comes to being suddenly widowed, a woman must fall
back on her own abilities to cope. The Amish adapt.

A young couple resided in Arthur, Illinois. She didn't
want me to use the real names for a book, so I will
name them William and Susan. William was a furniture
maker. He had always appeared healthy, but in 1962,
William had a blood vessel rupture in the brain causing
sudden death. Susan was only twenty-seven at the
time. She was left in shock with four small children,
two girls and two boys. The oldest was five and the
youngest was three months old.

After her husband's death, she did the only logical thing
and took over his furniture making business. The
employees, Amish men were taken by shock along with
Susan and realized what it must have been for her.
They pitched in and tried to do their job and help her to
give the business their top quality. With the help of her
employees, she managed to do well and her reputation
as a cabinet and furniture maker grew. Soon she had
more than enough business to take care of the family's
needs.

The one and only draw back to Susan was physical; she
had fallen out of a bed as young girl and injured her
head, neck, and shoulders. The heavy work of
furniture making began to aggravate those old injuries.
Since she was originally from Holmes County, Ohio,

she decided to have a sale and move back to her own hometown, where her family could give her a helping hand when needed.

Today she has two married children. The youngest is a boy who is working away. Her oldest child is a daughter and still living with her and they have a new business which requires much less strength than the furniture business, however, she is still known for her woodwork skills.

The mother and daughter business consists of sewing quilt tops. They both can make one quilt top in a day. They make long star tops. They do not finish the quilt but simply complete the quilt tops.

Each day they sit before a long row of windows which provide good natural light with treadle machine and agile hands and feet, making their own living.

This Amish widow not only had to overcome the difficulty of learning to be a first class cabinet maker, but when her own body failed her, she did not despair, but developed yet another talent. Doesn't the Amish way have a lot to teach us all about living?

1-881061-00

AMISH WOMEN

SMALL ENGINE REPAIR SHOP

While traveling across the United States, looking for unique Amish women, I was told of an Old Order Mennonite widow in the Elkhart, Indiana area, who had taken over her husband's small engine repair business when he was taken away from her through death.

The Old Order Mennonites are not akin to the Old Order Amish, but they too are horse and buggy people. They worship in a meeting house instead of their homes. In many ways they are similar to the Old Order, forsaking insurance as a lack of faith in God.

Mrs. Shrock, named Irene, was the oldest child from a family of eleven children. Her father was a blacksmith man and had his shop on the home place. She had taken an interest in her father's work as a child, asking him, "Why do you do this, and how do you do that?" These were her favorite questions as she was growing up. Her father was always patient with her and would answer and explain. Irene was her fathers' boy since they didn't have any boys in her family.

Irene, as a teenager met a young man and they were married in December of 1960. The young man started a small engine repair business in his parents basement before he married Irene. Later, they purchased a home and converted the garage into his place of business. They named it "**Shrocks Small Engine Sales and Repair**".

In the fourth year of their marriage they learned that he had one of the major man killer diseases (cancer). Two years had passed and the disease could not be defeated.

Mr. Schrock, was working eight hours a day away from the home and after dinner he would work at his business in the shop, Irene would join her husband after the dishes were done to spend time with him, while she still had him.

Mr. Schrock, was concerned for his family and asked her, "Would you want to take over the business when I leave?" She was lacking self-confidence and thought that she couldn't do it. He was thinking ahead and wanted to help his family be self-reliant.

Later one evening after dinner, Irene's husband asked her if she would come to the shop after she is done in the kitchen. When she went to the shop, he placed a lawn mower in front of her and said, "Fix this lawn mower", "Oh , I can't. "You can if you want to." "You can do anything that you set your mind to," he told her. 'I will direct you step by step." Irene started working on the lawn mower engine. When she tried to take a leaking seal out, it didn't want to come out. He looked over her shoulder and said "Just keep at it." Despite her frustration she kept at it and finally she got it off.

They worked side by side in the shop until he had taught her what he knew about small engines. While they worked together he would ask again and again "Do you want to take over the small engine repair business when I leave?" "I can't" she commented. "You can do anything you set your mind to", he replied, in his stern yet gentle voice.

88

1-881061-00

AMISH WOMEN

SMALL ENGINE REPAIR SHOP

After giving Irene two years of training in the small engine repair shop, her dear husband passed away. She was left with three little children to raise. However she had been trained in the small engine repair business by a man who would not take no for an answer.

There were times when her business was slow. Irene would bake on the side and sell her baked goods in the nearby communities, making her deliveries with her horse and buggy.

Wouldn't it be great if every man could teach his wife to work by his side and to take over his work if they depended on self-reliance rather than insurance or from community handouts like welfare? Today her mother lives with her since her father died, but she still maintains the business. Her motto is, "Just keep at it. I can do all things through Christ who strengthens me. Faith, love, and trust in Christ have been the Amish and Mennonites belief since the beginning."

Irene, is and excellent example for the Amish women in America. Isn't she quite an outstanding woman?"

1-881061-00

THE QUILT MAKERS

Quilt making started many years ago when mothers, wives, and young girls cut and sewed their own clothes. They would have bits and pieces of material left. They didn't believe in throwing anything away. They would sew the bits and pieces together and make quilt tops after they had accumulated bags and bags of materials in pieces.

They were too poor to throw anything away, if there was any way to make it useful. Some women were creative and made their own patterns for quilts.

An Amish woman may travel with husband to visit some of their family or friends in other states. If she sees a new quilt pattern she likes, she will ask for it and a pattern will be made for her to take along home for her use. Many of the patterns are handed down from generation to generation.

Today a single girl or widow will make quilts for her own independent income. Amish believe in taking care of themselves. However, they know they can depend on their fellow-man in times of need.

Mrs. Troyer, now of Topeka, Indiana is from a family of ten living children. She is the oldest, born in Reno County, Kansas. She stands only four feet and five inches tall. She lives with one of the nine children she bore during the years of her marriage and resides today in the Mummy Haus, she and her husband occupied in their last years. He died in 1987, by one of the major man killers in this country today. (Cancer)

1-881061-00

149332

LIST OF STATES AND TOWNS WHERE ALMA'S AMISH FAMILIES ARE EXPLODING IN AMERICA AND CANADA

OKLAHOMA
  Chouteau
PENNSYLVANIA
  Belleville
  Paradise
  Sandy Lake
  West Middlesex
SOUTH CAROLINA
  Westminister
TENNESSEE
  Lobelville
TEXAS
  Dalhart
  Flatonia
  Houston
  Lake Creek
  Shiner
VIRGINIA
  Chesapeake
  Ft. Lee
WISCONSIN
  Amherst
  Augusta
  Chetek
  Chile
  Coloma
  Curtiss
  Dalton
  Fairchild
  Granton
  Hancock
  LaFarge
  Pardeeville
  Tomah
  Watoma
  Wilton

1-881061-00

Mrs. Troyer refused the church's offer to help pay hospital expenses. "As long as I am able to pay the bills, I want to do it." She stated, " I quilt and I love to quilt, this is how I make payments.

When my mother Katie, and I stopped to visit a friend Mary, she was at the family house getting noon dinner and watching her grandchildren while her daughter-in-law was in the field picking corn to help her husband. Wives on the farm will jump right in to help their husbands to get the crops in before the cold winter sets in.

Although Mrs. Troyer invited us to dinner, we had other plans. When her son and daughter-in-law came in from the field, Grandma, refused to sit down and eat. She claimed she had more important things to do. She was happy to see her Aunt Katie, and said we had a lot of catching up to do. She insisted that we go over to her Mummy Haus, she wanted to show us her beautiful quilts, one was in the frame that she was working on.

While visiting with her, we asked about her husband. It was still a very tender subject. Tears came to her eyes, "For a long time it was hard to accept that my David is gone," she commented. I reminded her that she had her children. She said, "Yes, I would decay if I didn't have my children."

"Children are a blessing," Jesus said. It has been proven time and time again, in the Amish homes.

Today, the elderly women have their private little Dawdy and Mummy Haus, close to the family house.

The young family will help grandma and life doesn't stop, they are needed to help with the grandchildren.

The Amish believe parents take care of their children until they are grown up. Then the children get their turn taking care of the parents. Isn't this a wonderful way of life?

Some children like to play tricks on the grandparents. There was a family living in Nappanee, Indiana named Troyer. Grandma didn't know how to read the English language. She was four feet and eleven inches tall , and very petite. Grandma was always happy to see all the children and grandchildren come home.

One day Grandma, Mary Ann, wanted to go to town and her grandson volunteered to take her. He took her to Nappanee, and when they were going into town, Grandma noticed a new business had opened. She asked, "What kind of store is that?" "Oh, that is a new china and glass store." "Oh, really?" The Amish women really enjoy dishes and even some men like them. The Grandson Roy asked, "Would you like to go in to see them?" "OH YAH!" They walked over and Grandma started to walk in. Roy stated, "You have to pay to get in, but I will be happy to pay your way." "Nah, I can't believe they would make you pay to get into a store to see their dishes," she commented.

1-881061-00

AMISH WOMEN

THE QUILT MAKERS

"They are very expensive so they put a charge on it, to protect them and the dishes. I'll pay your way," Roy told Grandma, "if you want to see them." "Oh, alright." He paid her way. They went inside, she stated, "Oh, this is so different." "Grandma, sit here." "Why? " "Because, they will show them up there." Then the lights went out, music began to play and a picture came on. Grandma realized that Roy had played a trick on her, he jumped up trying to grab his crutches to get away from Grandma. She was after Roy, beating him with her purse all the way out to the street. Grandma was very upset, because Roy had taken her into a theater. The Amish don't believe in such. This story was told at the family get-together as long as she lived. Poor Grandma, lived to be ninety-two years of age and she never lost her ability to enjoy a good laugh.

1-881061-00

FAMILY CARE

When you drive through the Amish country you will
see that there are two houses on many Amish farms.
Many people have questioned me, "Are they so rich
that they have two houses?" Really to the contrary
some are rather poor

The grandparents will surrender the big family house
over to one of the children and the Grandparents will
move into the Dawdy Haus. (Grandpa's House.)

The children will take over the farm and the hard labor.
The Grandparents help with the farm. They don't quit
working. When Spring arrives Grandma is outside
helping plant garden with the others. She will help with
the cold packing for the cold winter months, assuring
themselves against hunger in the winter time.

When a child gets sick, Grandmother would guide them
to home remedies for recovery. Grandma would place
a clean diaper or a clean rag on the old wood stove to
warm up, while she rubs vicks on the chest and then
puts the warm material on the chest for colds. She
would mix some lemon and honey in a cup of hot water
to give the sick one to drink and put them to bed. A
warm towel or diaper would be put on the ears after a
few drops of sweet oil were put in the ears. For sick
stomach, tea is made of spearmint or catnip.

For kidney infection, tame carrot tops may be cut and
washed, cover with water in a pan, boil until water is
mint green, drink the tea. Four times a day required.

1-881061-00

AMISH WOMEN

Ma's salve. A salve that draws and keeps you from
getting blood poisoning.

Grandma's Salve

Mix:
2 handful bittersweet roots
1 oz. oregano oil
1 lb. Vaseline
2 oz. sweet oil

You fry the roots in Vaseline or you may use other fats
that get harder then Vaseline. (Crisco)

Grandchildren enjoy visiting Grandma's house because
she would have candy tucked away, she would always
give the children a piece. Sometimes, it would be some
of Grandma's homemade cookies.

When Grandpa turned the responsibility over to the
children they would travel more. My (the author)
Grandparents would come to visit and spend the
summer with us on the farm. They came to help us and
they enjoyed going fishing. This was a big help because
we lived on a farm with lots of wild game. At the end
of the day we would gather around to see what they
had caught.

A table was moved outside. The fish were placed on it
to be cleaned. One evening Grandma came home with
a giant turtle. We couldn't believe our eyes. She
warned us not to get too close. It might snap off our
fingers. Turtles can snap fingers off your hand.
Grandma was a big help in providing for some food
while she was at our house in the summer time visiting.

FAMILY CARE

The river ran through the woods and there was a big round area where you could see the giant snapping turtle. Grandma, made efforts and she caught one. When the fish was cleaned, we had a big fish-fry. The turtle was made into turtle soup.

Grandparents were always special to us, because they are special people.

However, many people miss out on their grandparents when they put them in a senior care center. They don't get to enjoy the stories of their experience and the kind things they can do for the family. Those little things bring joy and leave remembrances for the rest of our lives. Grandparents are appreciated and loved forever to an Amish family.

1-881061-00

DEATH

In the English world, death is postponed by every means possible; not only with all kinds of medication but all types of machines.

In the Amish world, death is accepted just as is birth. When it does come, it is not something that calls for tremendous grief. The Amish realize that the body is out of it's pain and suffering. The Soul will be judged on the judgment day, when Christ returns.

A just reward for a long virtuous life that was filled with hard work and devotion to the family and community. They are a community of customs. When a person is pronounced dead, the family is notified by a neighbor who has a telephone.

The Amish (Old Order Church) of the community will provide help with a person from each family. The meals are prepared and they will take care of the house and help with the children if needed, for three days or until the funeral is over. They will bring food for the family, usually enough for the guests. Leftovers will be served on the day of the funeral. The family that had the death will provide noodles and sandwiches for the families on the day of the funeral. They hope that the families will stay for dinner after the funeral so they can visit with them after the funeral is over.

After the funeral service, everyone will walk past the body to pay their last respects. The preacher will walk to the casket, after the last person passes and close it. The six boys or men, chosen to carry the casket to the funeral wagon, will walk to the casket, pick it up and

JOE E. GYODER
B. NOV 20 1868
D. JUNE 16 1921
A. 52 Y 5 M 23 D

MARIA YODER
B. JAN 8 1876
D. SEPT 14 1974

Anna M. Miller
B Feb 27 1871
D Oct 31 1926
a 55 yrs 8 mo 4 dys
M 1st to J S F Y
2nd to D J M

POLLY TROYER
B. MAR 30, 1937
D. APR 2, 1937

AMISH WOMEN

1-881061-00

carry it to the wagon. One of the six will drive the horse and wagon to the grave yard. The family follows them and there the last song and prayer is given before the casket is lowered into the ground and the dirt is put back into the hole. The boys or men that were chosen to carry the casket, will use shovels to put the dirt back. The family will sing songs until they are finished.

When the graveside service is over, every one returns to the house for dinner that has been prepared by the ladies of the community. The family enjoys being able to visit with so many of the friends and the families they haven't seen since the last funeral.

Mother always said, "you go to the funeral for the living, not for the dead. May the dead rest in peace."

AMISH WOMEN

A WOMAN

A woman's place is very dramatic. She has the greatest
of responsibilities. She was given more power than
man.

She is a bearer of life! She bears the child and
nourishes so it may grow.

She teaches the child to love God and man.

She lives to be an example for the child and teaches it
to be a leader.

She lives a simple life, her material treasures are
beautiful dishes displayed in her china cupboard or a
piece of fabric. She will use to make a quilt that will
show her hidden talents of excellent workmanship, to
be displayed on a bed to keep a body warm on a cold
winter night.

She is her husbands work-mate and his companion.

She shows her children how to live and then, how to
die, gracefully.

She will be gone but her life's accomplishments will live
on.

1-881061-00

AMISH WOMEN

AMISH WOMEN
P.O. BOX 375
DANVILLE, OH 43014-0375

Qty	Items	Price	Total
	AMISH WOMEN	$5.95	
	AMISH TASTE COOKING step by step	$4.95	
	AMISH LIFE THROUGH A CHILDS EYE	$6.95	
	ALMA'S AMISH KITCHEN	$10.95	
	ART OF AMISH COOKING	$10.95	
	ALPHABET IN AMISH LIFE	$2.25	
	AMISH DOLL (girl 17') each	$26.95	
	AMISH DOLL (boy 17") pair	$49.50	
Please add shipping & handling cost for dolls		$3.35	
Plus add shipping $2.40 for 1st book and $1.00 for each additional book. Ship U.P.S.			
Ohio residents add 5 1/2% sales tax.			
Total			

Ship to:

Name:
Address:
City, State, Zip Code:
Date:

ALL PRICES SUBJECT TO CHANGE

1-881061-00